TEXTILES

Susan Niner Janes

SEA-TO-SEA

Mankato Collingwood London

This edition first published in 2006 by
Sea-to-Sea Publications
1980 Lookout Drive
North Mankato
Minnesota 56003

Copyright © Sea-to-Sea Publications 2006

Printed in China

Library of Congress Cataloging-in-Publication Data

Janes, Susan Niner.
    Textiles/ by Susan Niner Janes.
        p. cm. – (Art and craft skills)
    Includes index.
    ISBN 1-932889-86-8
        1. Textile crafts–Juvenile literature. I. Title. II. Art
    and craft skills (North Mankato, Minn.)

TT699.J36 2005
746–dc22   2004062737

9 8 7 6 5 4 3 2

Published by arrangement with the Watts Publishing Group Ltd., London

Franklin Watts and the
author wish to thank the
following manufacturers for
supplying craft materials used
in making the projects in this
book:
Ribbons courtesy of Offray Ribbon
Rainbow Felt courtesy of Kunin
Felt

Series editor: Kyla Barber
Designer: Lisa Nutt
Illustrator: Lynda Murray
Photographer: Steve Shott
Art director: Robert Walster

Contents

Getting Started

Textiles—fibers, fabrics, and thread—can be painted, dyed, woven, wrapped, sewn, knotted, glued, and even molded. The projects in this book introduce a whole range of textile crafts.

Which Stitch?

A few of the projects in this book require basic sewing skills. If you don't already know how, practice these easy stitches.

Running Stitch—the basic stitch for joining two pieces of fabric together.

1. Thread needle and knot the end of your thread. Push needle to the front of the fabric, from the back. Pull thread up until the knot tugs.

2. A little farther along, push the needle back down. Continue sewing in and out, making even stitches.

3. When you reach the end, sew around and around through the last stitch, then cut off the thread.

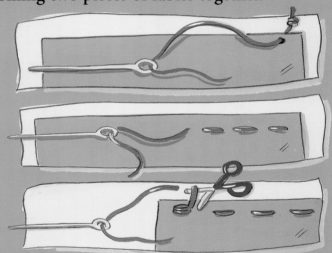

Oversewing—to neaten an edge or join two fabrics together at their edges.

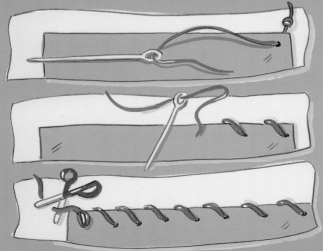

1. Thread needle and knot the end of the thread. Push needle through from the back of the fabric to the front.

2. Loop the needle over the edge and up through the back again. Continue looping around and around, making slanted stitches.

3. When you reach the end, sew around and around through the last stitch, then cut off the thread.

Blanket Stitch—to neaten an edge or join two fabrics together at their edges.

1. Thread needle, knot thread end. Bring needle up on front of fabric, then push it back through a little to the right, away from fabric edge.

2. Hold needle straight and pass it through the loop. Keep stitching in this way toward the right, always passing the needle through the loop.

3. Try to space your stitches evenly. When you reach the end, stitch around and around through the last stitch, then cut off thread.

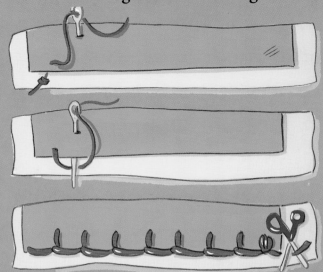

Note: The stitches are shown for right-handers, left-handers sew in the opposite direction.

Finishing Knot
Tie a knot on the wrong side of the fabric:

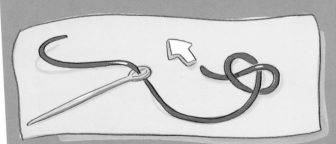

Joining Knot
To change thread color as you sew:

Pinning
To pin fabric to hold it together as you stitch it in place:

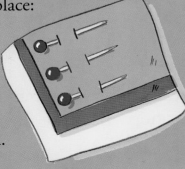

◎ Pin at right angles to the fabric edge, if there is room. The pin points should face inward.

◎ Remove the pins as soon as you have finished stitching. Put them back in their container—and shut the lid.

◎ You can also use masking tape or safety pins to hold fabric together temporarily. Sometimes paper clips will work along fabric edges.

Textile Supplies

Materials for textile crafts are not difficult to find—but you have to know where to look for them. The store key will help.

Store Key

Art supply store

Craft store

Fabric store

Yarn store

Supermarket

Sewing Kit

1. Scissors—you need sharp ones for cutting fabric, so be very careful and ask an adult for help if necessary. It is useful to have a big pair and a small pair, so you can handle all sorts of cutting jobs.

2. Pinking shears cut fabric in a zigzag edge and stop it from fraying.

3. Safety pins for a safer way to pin.

4. Straight pins can be used for keeping fabrics in place while you are putting your project together.

5. Needles—you will need two kinds of large-eyed needles: tapestry needles (with blunt tips) and embroidery needles (with pointy tips). Also some ordinary sewing needles. Store needles through a scrap of felt when they are not in use.

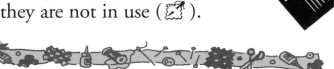

Fabric, Yarn, and Thread

6. Felt is a nonwoven textile material. It comes in a wide range of colors and will not fray. Some felt is washable.

7. Fabric can be woven, non-woven, knitted, printed, or plain. Look for interesting textures and try to recycle old clothes.

8. Net is good for see-through designs; it comes in many colors.

9. Bulky knitting yarn is good for quick results, and tapestry wool works well for finer projects.

10. Soft embroidery thread for easy sewing. Use embroidery cotton strands for details.

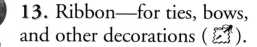

Bits and Pieces

11. Fiberfill stuffing for soft toy filling ( ).

12. Batting comes in a flat sheet. Use it as a filling material, for padding ( ).

13. Ribbon—for ties, bows, and other decorations ( ).

14. Beads, buttons, sequins, and feathers for decoration ( ).

15. Goggle eyes can be glued on soft toys ( ).

Art Box

16. Masking tape can often be used instead of pins ( ).

17. White glue can be thinned with water and used as a coating. Remember—it's not washable ( ).

18. Acrylic paints can be used on fabric ( ).

19. A variety of paintbrushes ( ).

20. Cold-water dyes: You need a pack of dye fix for each box of dye ( ).

21. Fabric paints—always read the label on the jar or tube ( ).

22. Dimensional fabric paint for making raised outlines ( ).

23. Steel ruler ( ).

24. Pencils and erasers ( ).

25. Paper, cardboard, and oaktag ( ).

26. Sticky putty ( ).

27. Plasticine—for sculpting molds for fabric mâché ( ).

From the Kitchen

Waxed paper—low-cost tracing paper ( ).

Dried rice or lentils for filling juggling bags ( ).

Plastic bowl or margarine tub—dye containers ( ).

Liquid detergent for cleaning up ( ).

Plastic drinking straws for curling ribbon ( ).

Table salt used for dyeing ( ).

Plastic food wrap to stop wet material from sticking ( ).

Keep It Tidy!

Paper towels or rags for wiping spills.
Newspapers—to cover tabletops.
Old clothes—to wear for messy projects.

Rag Craft

Rag craft projects usually start with fabric strips or scraps. Recycle old clothes and pieces of spare material and create something new from something old.

You Will Need

- three colors of felt
- ribbon
- scraps of fabric
- embroidery needle
- scissors
- net (to match felt)
- embroidery thread
- straight pins
- dried lentils or rice
- pencil and ruler

1. For each juggling bag cut two 4 x 4-inch (10 x 10-cm) squares of felt and two 4 x 4-inch (10 x 10-cm) squares of net in a matching color. Then cut small pieces of ribbon, fabric, and embroidery thread.

2. Arrange the rag scraps on a felt square. Place a net square over the felt square and pin, then sew, edges together, sandwiching the rag scraps in between. Repeat for the other pieces of felt and net.

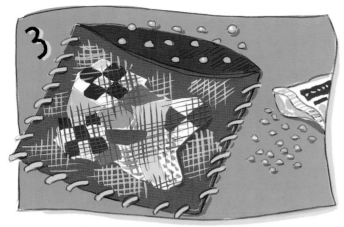

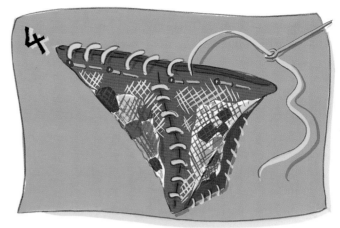

3. Pin the squares together. Oversew three sides, then fill about three-quarters full with dried lentils or rice.

4. Squeeze the two unsewn edges of the bag together so the seams are in the center. This makes a pyramid shape. Pin in place, then oversew to seal.

Now Try These

Rag-Knot Picture Frames

To make a rag knot, just cut fabric into strips, knot each tightly three times, then cut off the tail. This forms a ball. To make up, cut a frame from a cardboard box, then glue lots of knots onto the frame to create a pattern.

Rag-Wrapped Bangles

Cut a strip of plastic from a soda drink's bottle. Wrap sharp edges with masking tape and tape plastic into a ring. Cut a strip of batting and glue it on. Cut rag strips and spiral them around to cover the bracelet base, knotting rags to join on new colors.

TEXTILE TIPS

◆ Net can be slippery to use. An easy way to cut net is to stick masking tape onto the net to make the shape, then cut along the tape edges.

◆ Combine plain and patterned rags in your projects. When knotted, patterned rags have a speckled appearance.

◆ Rags are also just what you need for the craft of fabric mâché (see page 20), and for making decorative patches on clothing (see page 11).

Appliqué

Appliqué is a technique of adding patches and trimmings to pictures and clothes. Recycle old material and try this fabric art picture.

1. Plan your design on paper. An appliqué picture is sewn on in layers, so you must think carefully about the shapes of the pieces and the order in which they have to be sewn on.

2. Trace pattern shapes onto some waxed paper, then cut them out. Number the waxed paper shapes with their sewing order. Pin each one to your chosen fabric, then cut it out.

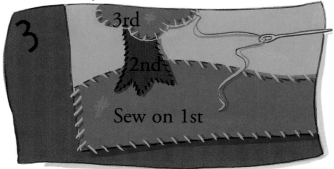

3. Pin, then sew each piece of fabric onto the background fabric (the blue felt) in the numbered order. Use decorative embroidery stitches, such as oversewing or the blanket stitch (see pages 4–5).

4. Add the finishing touches: sew or glue on beads for "apples" and a doorknob; paint the windowpanes; sew flower stems and sew or glue on button flowers.

Now Try These

Patterned Denim

Cut out denim shapes, then wash them to "fray" the edges. Ask an adult to iron them. Sew patches on and decorate them as shown.

Star T-Shirt

Take an old T-shirt and cut out a star shape in the center. Wash and dry the T-shirt to fray the cutout edges. Pin a big patch of fabric behind the opening and sew it in place.

TEXTILE TIPS

◎ Appliqué can be glued instead of sewn. Use textile glue, for washable results.

◎ To stop ribbon ends from fraying when you cut them, brush with watered-down white glue.

Simple Shisha

This method is inspired by the shisha mirror embroidery of India and Pakistan, in which real mini-mirrors are stitched onto fabric.

You Will Need

- ★ metallic cardboard
- ★ white glue (optional)
- ★ thick paper (optional)
- ★ fine-point pen
- ★ wool or cotton embroidery thread
- ★ large-eyed embroidery needle
- ★ sharp pencil or nail
- ★ backing fabric
- ★ sticky putty
- ★ scissors ★ a coin

1. If your metallic cardboard is thin, glue a piece of thick paper onto the back. Draw around a coin to make mirror disks. Cut them out.

2. Place the mirror disk on top of a blob of sticky putty. Push a sharp pencil or nail through each disk four times. The putty will catch the sharp point.

3. Put the mirror disk on backing fabric and hold it in place with your thumb. Bring the needle and thread up from under the fabric and sew through the holes, working your way around the mirror. Tie thread ends at the back.

Backpack and Purse

A drawstring bag is a traditional shisha project—you could also add straps to make a backpack. Each bag is made from two felt rectangles—you only have to decorate the front.

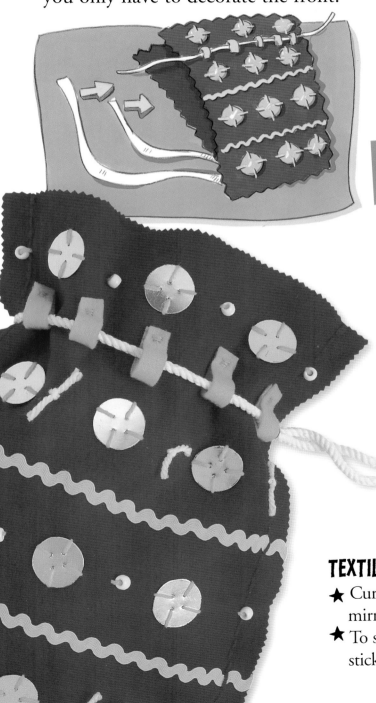

What Next?

A shape with four center holes can be stitched on in several different ways:

Now Try These

Night Sky Pencil Case

Cut out stars and planets from metallic cardboard. Pierce one hole in the center of each. Sew into the hole from each edge using metallic thread.

Baseball Cap

Sew shapes onto a baseball cap. You can even create patterned shapes by gluing computer clip art or magazine cuttings onto cardboard and stitching it on.

TEXTILE TIPS

★ Curved nail scissors make easy work of cutting out mirror disks (ask permission before using them).
★ To stop your "mirrors" moving as you sew them, stick them in place with white glue.

Sock Toys

Make soft toys easily and simply by stuffing the toe end of an old sock and adding stiffened ribbon for hair. Add felt details and goggle eyes to make different characters.

1. Cut off the toe end of an old sock. Stuff it, then sew a running stitch close to the cut edge. Pull up the thread ends and knot them.

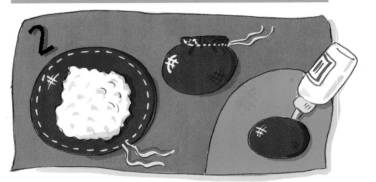

2. For a nose, cut a circle from the sock. Stitch around the edge leaving loose ends and put stuffing in the center. Pull up the thread, knot the ends, and glue in place.

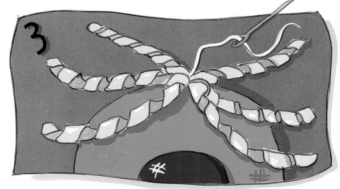

3. For the hair, make stiffened ribbon spirals and zigzags as shown opposite. Cut three pieces of the curly ribbon, cross them at their centers, and sew on.

4

4. Cut felt pieces for the hands and feet and glue them in place. Hold the felt pieces as the glue dries. Glue on eyes and paint a mouth with fabric paint.

Curly Ribbon

For spirals, wind ribbon around a plastic drinking straw (hold ends in place with tape) and brush with water-thinned white glue. Let dry. For zigzags, wind ribbon around a 0.5-in. (1cm-) wide strip of oaktag, which has been covered with plastic food wrap and brush with water-thinned white glue.

Now Try These

Penguins

Make bodies from black socks, then glue on a felt bib, beak, fish, wings, feet, and goggle eyes. You can also add a ribbon bow tie.

Pocket-sized Toys

Cut out a shape in oaktag, cut a piece of batting the same size and stick it to the oaktag. Cover in the leftover sock material and decorate. Make badges, hair ties, or refrigerator magnets.

TEXTILE TIP

• To stop your sock toy from wobbling, glue oaktag to the bottom of the feet.

Weaving

These sports fans are made using needle weaving on oaktag. You can weave all kinds of thread in this way to create all kinds of effects.

You will need

- ★ yarn
- ★ colored felt
- ★ colored oaktag
- ★ sticky putty
- ★ dimensional fabric paint
- ★ sharp pencil or nail
- ★ white glue
- ★ tapestry needle
- ★ paintbrush   ★ ruler
- ★ acrylic paint

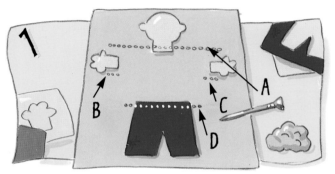

1. Cut out felt head, arms, and jeans; glue them onto some oaktag. Pierce holes about 1/4 of an inch (5mm) apart with a sharp pencil or nail. Pierce 20 holes at A, 3 at B, 3 at C, and 14 at D.

2. Thread a needle with yarn, and knot the end. Bring the needle to the front of the card through hole E and back down through F. Continue weaving the yarn through all the holes. Knot on the back.

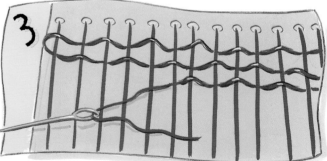

3. Thread the needle and knot the end. Bring the needle up below hole E and weave it "over then under" to the left. Reverse the weaving direction at the row end; weave "under then over" across the second row.

4. Weave until you reach the bottom, then bring the yarn to the back and knot it. Glue on felt details—some hair and a badge, and paint on a face.

Now Try These

Woven Ribbon

Pin eight rows of ribbons on to the "sticky" side of a piece of iron-on interfacing. Weave eight strands of a different color of ribbon across them. Sew a running stitch around the edges through all the layers to keep them in place. Ask an adult to iron the weaving. Trim the weaving close to the stitching. Tape the woven ribbon behind an oaktag cutout.

Sporty Scarves

Make a scarf in your team colors and attach it to your sports fan. You can make a scarf out of an old sock, felt, paper, yarn, or ribbon.

TEXTILE TIP

★ Experiment with different wools, textures, and colors.

Friendship Chains

Friendship chains are quick and easy to make from simple links. Use small links for bracelets or larger ones for belts and handles. Experiment with colors, materials, and fabrics.

You Will Need

- ★ felt
- ★ oaktag
- ★ tracing paper
- ★ fine-point pen
- ★ beads or tassels (optional)
- ★ pencil ★ needle and thread
- ★ masking tape
- ★ narrow ribbon ★ scissors

Link Pattern

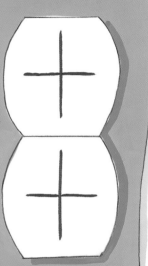

This is the template for one bracelet-sized chain link. Cut slits on the red lines for plaited-look chains and on the blue lines for disk-link chains. For belt links, enlarge the template.

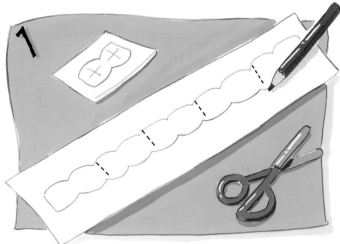

1. A template for the basic bracelet link is given above. Trace it onto oaktag and cut it out. Draw around this shape, end to end, five times on a long piece of oaktag. Cut it out and tape it onto a piece of felt.

2. Draw around the oaktag edge with a fine-point pen and cut out the strip of felt. To cut the strip into links, just snip across at the narrow part, every two bumps. Repeat using felt of different colors.

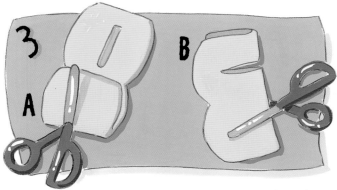

3. For a plaited-look chain, cut the slits as shown above in A. To make a disk-link chain, cut the slits as shown in B.

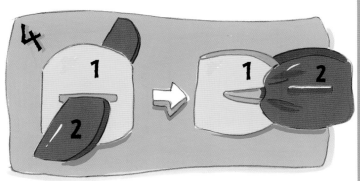

4. Fold link 1 in half widthwise. Fold link 2 in half lengthwise, thread it through slits of link 1. Now spread the two halves of link 2 open and fold them together as you did for link 1. This makes a new link. Repeat to build up your chain. Sew on ribbons, beads, or tassels.

Now Try These

Neck Purse
For each side of the purse, make three five-link chains. Oversew them together, side to side. Pin front and back together and oversew the edges, leaving top open. Sew on a ribbon strap.

Bag Straps
Cut a large rectangle of burlap. Make chain-link straps and sew them on. Fold the burlap in half and sew the sides together. You can fringe the edges of the burlap.

Fabric Mâché

Fabric mâché and papier-mâché are similar crafts. Paste small pieces of fabric over a mold, or base, to build up a shape. Try this lion mask—it's light and slightly bendy.

You Will Need

- lightweight fabric, cut into small rectangles, about (1.5 x 2 in.) 4cm x 5cm • plasticine
- a large piece of cardboard • white glue
- acrylic paints • 12 in. (30cm) of black cord elastic
- paintbrushes • plastic food wrap
- scissors • pencil • nail for piercing

1. Sketch a lion mask on thick cardboard. Build up the nose, mouth, and eyebrow areas with plasticine. Cover it all with plastic food wrap.

2. Soak the fabric rectangles in white glue thinned with water. Place them on the mask mold one at a time, overlapping them. Shape them to the mold.

3. For the mane, stick fabric pieces to the outer edges of the mask shape. Let it dry in a warm place. Lift the mask off the mold and cut out eyeholes.

4. Replace the mask on the mold and paint it. Let it dry. Brush on a layer of watery white glue for a shiny finish. Pierce holes at the sides with a pencil and tie on elastic cord.

Now Try These

Patchwork Bowls
Cut squares of gingham fabric, and mold them over a bowl covered in plastic food wrap. When the fabric is dry, varnish with white glue. Pierce evenly spaced holes around top. Work a blanket stitch or oversewing through the holes.

TEXTILE TIPS
◎ Choose lightweight fabrics to get a slightly see-through effect.
◎ Unlike papier-mâché, a single layer of fabric mâché is all you need. Make sure that fabric pieces overlap without gaps.

Wrapping

Wrapping is where some wool is spiraled around an inner bundle of yarn to make a smooth covering. It adds strength and color to these wool people.

You Will Need

- bulky wool yarn ◆ cardboard ◆ ruler ◆ felt
- dimensional fabric paint ◆ scissors ◆ tapestry needle

Wrapping: The Basics

1. Make a wool loop as long as the section to be wrapped. Hold the loop in place with your thumb, then bring one wool end under and around the yarn you want to wrap.

2. Now spiral the wool around the yarn bundle, moving toward the loop.

3. Thread the "wrapping wool" through the loop.

4. Gently tug the bottom wool end until the loop and the wrapping yarn are pulled out of sight beneath the wrapping.

5. Snip off the wool tail at top. The wrapping will not come undone.

Simple Tassel

Cut a piece of cardboard. Wrap yarn around it, eight times or more. Tie the yarn ends tightly at the top and tuck the knot under. Cut through the bottom of the loops to free the tassel from the cardboard.

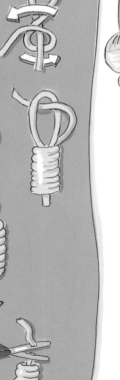

1. To make woolen dolls, cut a piece of cardboard 6 in. (15cm) long. Wrap yarn around it twenty times. Tie yarn at the top. Divide the tassel into two bunches of ten strands for the legs. Tie each bunch tightly at the bottom. Slip the tassel off the cardboard.

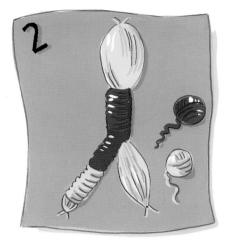

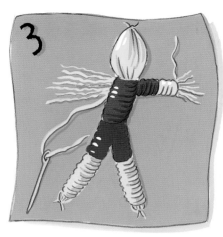

2. Start wrapping 1 in. (2.5cm) down from the top of the tassel. Wrap around the whole tassel for the body. In a new color, wrap one leg, then the other.

3. For the arms, cut eight wool strands 6 in. (15cm) long. Thread a needle with one strand and pass it through the body top. Repeat for all the strands, then wrap them to make arms.

4. To finish, stuff the head with some crumpled yarn. Cut across the loops at the leg bottoms. Trim arm ends. Add wool hair and paint a face with fabric paint.

Now Try These

Skipping Rope
Wrap a skipping rope in different colors. Paint the handles and add a wrapped yarn "grip" on each. Decorate with tassels (see page 22).

Beads
To make each bead, cut a strip of felt and fold it in half widthwise. Wrap the center section, then fringe the bottom edges. Decorate with fabric paint.

23

Wrap Weaving

These colorful weavings are inspired by *ojo de Dios* or "God's eyes"— Mexican folk-art symbols believed to bring good luck.

Hexagons

Draw a circle with a compass on oaktag. Keep the compass set to the same radius as your circle, then mark six points around the circle edge. Use a ruler and pencil to connect the points.

You Will Need

- ★ bulky wool yarn in different colors
- ★ large-eyed embroidery needle   ★ sharp pencil or nail
- ★ ruler and pencil   ★ sticky putty
- ★ scissors   ★ compass   ★ masking tape
- ★ colored oaktag

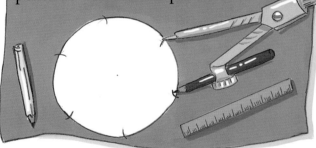

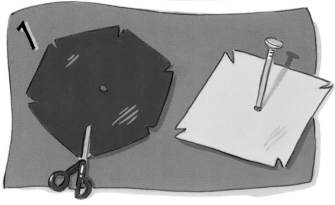

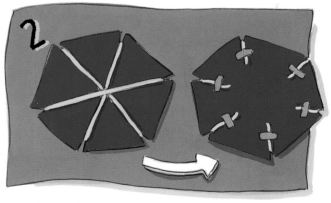

1. Cut squares and hexagons from the oaktag. Cut narrow slits in the corners, about 0.5 in. (1cm) deep. Carefully pierce a hole in the center of each card.

2. Thread the wool yarn through the slits as shown. The wool should be stretched tight. Tape the ends onto the back of the oaktag.

24

3. Thread a needle with your first color. Bring it up at the center, over the crossed yarns in the middle, then back down. Knot on the back. Then bring the yarn back up and loop it around each of the fixed wool spokes in turn.

4. To change colors, push the needle through the card at a wool spoke. Tie on a new color on the wrong side. Thread the needle, bring the wool back through the same hole to the right side, and continue weaving. To finish, tie on tassels (see page 22) and a hanging loop.

"Ojo" Colors
Ojo colors have meanings. Yellow stands for the sun god, green represents new life and growth, while blue is the rain god's color.

Now Try These

Holiday Sparkle
Take two cocktail or lollipop sticks, cross them at their centers and bind them together. Using a mixture of metallic and plain thread, weave by looping thread around each stick spoke in turn (no needle required). To finish, tie the end of the yarn onto one of the stick spokes. Glue beads onto the stick tips.

Weave a Web
The web is woven like the oaktag weavings, but the yarn is spaced apart. Make the creepy crawly from a rolled-up strip of fake-fur fabric and pipe cleaners.

25

Rosettes

Stitch a strip of fabric, pull up the thread and you have a flowerlike gathered circle called a rosette. Use rosettes as the building blocks for this bumble bee.

You will need

- 2 in. (5cm) –diameter polystyrene ball (from craft shops) ⊚ yellow net ⊚ old black sock
- yellow felt, black felt ⊚ needle and thread
- 20 in. (50cm) of black cord elastic
- 5 black beads ⊚ red stretchy fabric (for nose)
- furry pipe cleaners: 2 yellow, 4 black
- pinking shears ⊚ 2 goggle eyes
- scrap of red felt (for mouth) ⊚ white glue

Basic Rosette

Cut a strip of felt. For a decorative edge, cut the bottom of the strip with pinking shears. Sew a running stitch along the top edge, then pull together the loose ends of the thread to gather up the material.

Bumble Bee

1. To make a head, gather the heel of a sock over a polystyrene ball. Sew or glue on a red nose (see page 14). Sew on pipe cleaner antennae and glue on goggle eyes and a felt mouth. Sew on 20 in. (50cm) of cord elastic to the back of the head.

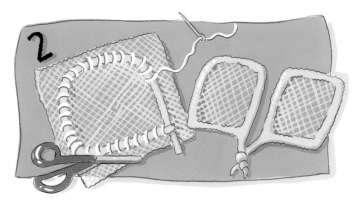

2. For wings, bend yellow pipe cleaners into loops. Lay them on top of a double layer of yellow net. Sew the net to each wing loop, then trim the edges. Twist wings together at the bottom to make a pair.

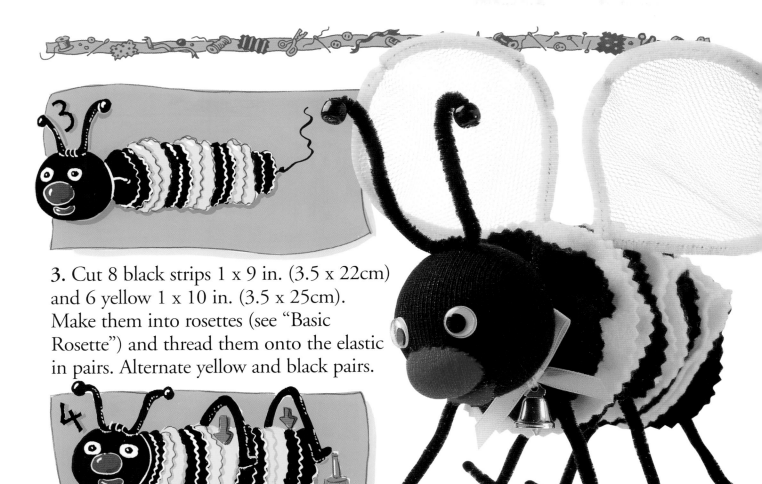

3. Cut 8 black strips 1 x 9 in. (3.5 x 22cm) and 6 yellow 1 x 10 in. (3.5 x 25cm). Make them into rosettes (see "Basic Rosette") and thread them onto the elastic in pairs. Alternate yellow and black pairs.

4. Bend three black pipe cleaners in half to make three pairs of legs. Slot them between the rosettes and glue them in place.

TEXTILE TIP

⊚ To make rosettes out of material other than felt, brush white glue, mixed with water, onto the fabric where you want to cut it. The edge will then be easier to cut and it won't fray.

Now try these

Glitzy Rosette
Make a winner's rosette by sewing net strips in two widths together as one rosette. Top this with a fabric rosette. Add a ribbon tail, sequins, and a safety pin fastener at the back.

Flower Garland Scarf
Sew fabric rosettes side by side and add felt leaves and bead "flower centers."

Resist Dyeing

Resist dyeing means that patterns are created by stopping dye or paint from soaking into the fabric evenly. Different things can be used to block out areas of color—here we use tying and masking tape.

You Will Need

- ★ for each color: a box of cold-water fabric dye; a pack of cold-water dye fix; and 2 ounces (60g) of table salt
- ★ old cotton hankies
- ★ measuring pitcher
- ★ plastic bowl
- ★ rubber gloves
- ★ tapestry wool
- ★ string and elastic bands
- ★ old spoon
- ★ scissors
- ★ plastic bags and ties
- ★ embroidery needle

1. Make the hankies damp and tie them to make patterns. Spotty: Tie in pebbles with string, very tightly. Stripes: Accordion fold the hankie and wrap it tightly with elastic bands. Bull's eye: Pick up the hankie by its center and crunch it into folds. Tie it tightly from the top down.

DYES ARE POWERFUL CHEMICALS. ASK AN ADULT TO HELP.

2. Ask an adult to prepare the dye solution in a plastic bowl and follow the manufacturer's instructions. Dunk the hankies in the dye and squeeze them lightly. After one minute, remove hankies and put them in a plastic bag. Leave overnight.

3. Next day, rinse the hankies under cold water until the water runs clear. Cut off the string or remove the elastic bands. Wash the hankies in hot water mixed with detergent liquid. Let them dry. Ask an adult to iron them.

4. Parachutes: Make wrapped doll sky divers (see page 22). Sew a piece of string on each corner of the hankie. Sew the free end of each string onto the sky diver's back.

Now Try These

Masking Tape Resist
Tape a triangle of dry fabric onto a piece of cardboard covered with plastic food wrap. Stick on pieces of masking tape, making a pattern. Brush on fabric paint mixed with water. Dry it in sunlight, then fix the color as directed. Use to make Windsurfers.

Paint Magic

Brush it, sponge it, squeeze it on—paints can transform a plain piece of fabric simply and easily.

You Will Need

- interfacing or lightweight fabric
- dimensional fabric paint
- fabric paints
- paintbrush
- oaktag
- pencil
- masking tape
- scissors
- white glue

Which Paint?

Fabric paints can be transparent (see-through), opaque (solid), or dimensional. To select a paint, first decide what effect you want to create, then read the labels to find out which paint can do the job. If you are still not sure which paint to buy, don't guess—ask a store clerk for advice.

Fat Cats

Draw a cat in pencil on some interfacing. Paint the outline using dimensional fabric paint. Next day, color in the "fur" with fabric paint. For a fuzzy effect, make the fabric damp before you start painting. Glue the cat onto some oaktag and cut it out.

Cave Painting

Paint background on wet fabric using fabric paints. When dry, paint on the animals.

Brilliant Butterflies

Paint butterflies on very wet interfacing. Dot the paint on with a brush—the color will spread. Try to make both wings match. Dry flat, then paint in the body with 3–D fabric paint.

Apple Bookmark

From a clear plastic folder, cut out an apple and a leaf shape to make two stencils. Cut a narrow strip of burlap. Tape the apple stencil onto the burlap and dab paint through the opening with a nearly dry brush. Do the apples first, then the leaves. Finally, paint on the stems. Cut a piece of felt and sew it to the back of the burlap.

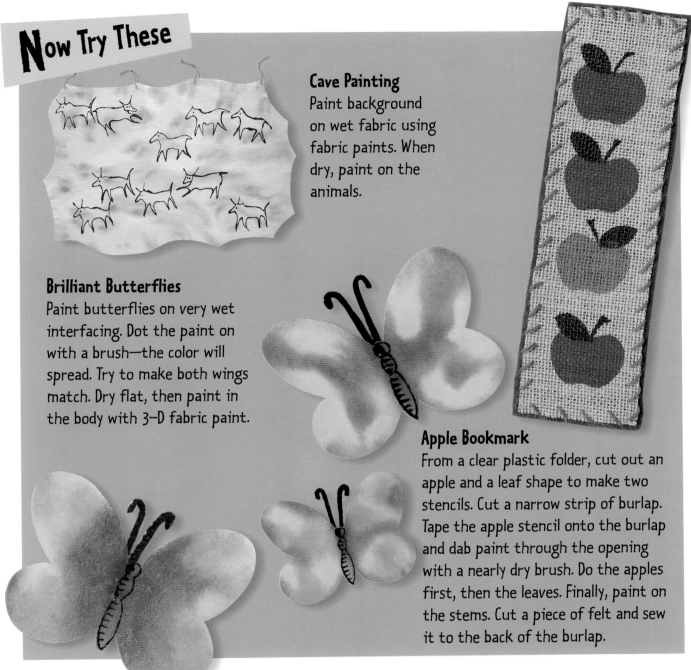

TEXTILE TIPS

◆ Always paint on natural fabrics, like 100 percent cotton, that have been washed first.

◆ Acrylic paints work well on fabric—but the results will be slightly stiffer than fabric paint, and they may not be washable.

◆ Try fabric crayons. Draw your design on paper, then have an adult iron it onto fabric. The flip image prints.

◆ Create an airbrush effect: mix creamy paint, then flick it onto fabric using an old toothbrush.

Glossary

appliqué Decorating fabric by attaching patches and trimmings (10–11).

batting A flat, fluffy sheet of fibers, similar to stuffing, which is used as padding (14–15).

fabric mâché A craft technique in which small pieces of fabric are glued together over a mold in order to construct a new object (20–21).

friendship bracelet A handmade bracelet, made as a gift. The giver ties it onto the friend's wrist as a symbol of friendship (18–19).

link A piece of a chain that fits together with other pieces that are exactly the same (18-19).

ojo de Dios A Mexican good-luck symbol, made of yarn wrapped around crossed sticks (24–25).

resist dyeing Any kind of fabric decoration in which areas of the fabric are prevented from soaking up dye or paint to make a pattern (28–29).

rosette A circle of fabric made from a strip that has been gathered along one long edge (26–27).

shisha A traditional style of Indian and Pakistani embroidery in which mirror disks are stitched onto fabric (12–13).

weaving A way of making fabric by lacing yarns together. Usually a set of yarns are set up, and then other yarns are inserted through or around them (16–17, 24–25).

wrapping A way of spiraling a piece of yarn around an inner bundle of yarns, making a smooth outer covering (22–23).

Index